Get It Together

Get It Together

✦

Long-distance relationship

Ermitha Gracia

iUniverse, Inc.
New York Lincoln Shanghai

Get It Together
Long-distance relationship

iUniverse books may be ordered through booksellers or by contacting:

iUniverse
2021 Pine Lake Road, Suite 100
Lincoln, NE 68512
www.iuniverse.com
1-800-Authors (1-800-288-4677)

ISBN-13: 978-0-595-39647-4 (pbk)
ISBN-13: 978-0-595-84051-9 (ebk)
ISBN-10: 0-595-39647-X (pbk)
ISBN-10: 0-595-84051-5 (ebk)

Printed in the United States of America

This book dedicates to everyone who is away from his or her soul mates or in process of going away for necessary reasons. For those who choose to put their dreams and plans on hold for someone else, those who are confuse on finding the right person to spend their lives with, those who are wasting times on a guy or female who doesn't even appreciate them, and for those who are looking down on other people and countries.

Contents

Introduction

Come-on, are you ready to encourage yourself to manage your future? Are you having difficulties making a decision that can change your life? Are you experiencing difficulties searching for the right one? Not ready to settle down with someone special? Do not know how to make a relationship work? Not really sure of what and who you really need in your life?

Do you do things to make yourself happy or do you do things to make other people happy? Do you feel you have to do things or do you feel you need to do what's important? Having problem knowing when you're ready to make serious decisions? Have you made any mistakes that, you wish you can go back and erase? Having problems letting things go?

Well; this book will encourage you to focus on you and encourage you to except changes. This book is the key to opening your eyes and finding your true self, and it shows how to keep yourself on board. I hope my Personal experiences show you how it's better to take your time instead of rushing into things, especially when we're not ready in general. I tried to make this book very easy to read and straight to my point. I certainly hope this book can be useful to you.

Chapter 1

To own it you have to work for it

God gives me a mind to understand when it comes on spending my life with a guy that guy has to have his head on his shoulder. By saying he has to respect my decisions, trust me and be supportive.

Just to let you know, when I knew I was ready for a serious relationship, I had stop using my emotions and I started using my heart. But before I give my heart to that person, I test him just to see if he has what it takes to be given my heart to and finding out if he worth for me to spend my life with or if he even wants to spend his life with me.

The reason why I choose to test my relationship is only because, sometime, someone can say they love you but have no idea what love means. Honestly; he/she probably really loves you from his/her heart, body, soul and mind, and at the same time he/she probably loves you because of your beauty or for what they think they can benefit from you.

True love does not have anything to do with beauty or vanities. Therefore I choose to test my relationship to find out more about that person. What happened after I find out what I needed to find out in that person? Well let just say I stop wasting my time, because there's no point of staying in a relationship with someone who doesn't deserve you.

I just think it's a good idea to test your mate just to find out if you can picture yourself with that person for the rest of your life. Test them to find out if they truly care for you, how they will approach you when they're upset, how their attitude and their behavior toward you when they're having a bad day and to find out if they have what it takes to be patient. However; never go over board with the testing, still show affection to your mate, because you don't want them thinking that you don't care or you're being selfish.

<u>Truth is</u>

I know for a fact that a long-distance relationship can get hard on some people. At the same time I believe if you have already made-up your mind to be with that person and you both are committed to each other then long distance relationship will not be a big issue. Not that I disagree with those who refuse to believe in long-distance relationships, however I'm certain that when someone's devoted to each other everything is possible. It just won't work, if one of them is the only one who's willing to work with the long-distance.

On the other hand, I think to deal with a long distance relationship you must be ready for a serious relationship. I'm talking about able to commit yourself to your mate. Able to say to yourself this person is the only one you can picture yourself with no matter what or no matter how far one of you may have to be sometime. Like I said; before you can ever think that way you must be ready for a serious relationship.

Chapter 2

Personal experience

I'm about to talk to you from personal experiences; I started having serious relationship in 1997. My first serious relationship was with a guy name Jerry. Jerry and I were living in Brooklyn, NY where we first met. After a while my parents and I had to relocate to Philadelphia, Pennsylvania, therefore I had to move from New York. Even when I moved from New York, we made time to visit each other.

Jerry was a nice guy, but my problem with him was, I felt he was holding my back from chasing my goals and his jealousy. Maybe yes; when a man or a woman gets jealous for you it shows that he/she cares, but only if he/she knows how to manage it. It's also very dangerous, when a man or a woman gets jealous, especially when they cannot control it. Sometimes it can means two things either they're crazy or insecure even when it hard for them to admit it.

And of course; We had try to find solution for that matter. He tried to change; he pretend for a couple months but then goes back in his same old way. He pretended for a couple of months, then after a while he started acting the same way he used to. Since then I knew it was not something Jerry can change, because this is who he was "**A Jealous man**" Therefore we just had to end the relationship, so that he could find his lady that can actually be satisfy with his ways and for me to find my man. Beside you should never force yourself or someone else to do or to stay in something they do not feel comfortable with.

Anyway, Jerry was so jealous that I could not have any friends calling my phone without him having any ideas. I could not travel by myself, which means; when I planned to go somewhere or do something if he's not capable to keep me company or didn't agree with what I would want to do then to him I should not go or do it.

But me; as an independent woman and me as a woman who wants to be my own person could not deal with situation like this. I would still go take care what I know is best for me, and every time I do that he would find a problem with it. Do not get me wrong; there was no physical abuse or verbal abuse. It just that "he would get upset by not talking to me and complained a lot when I won't let him control"

After I graduated on my first degree in Medical Office Management in Philadelphia, Pennsylvania, I wanted to take a year and couples months off from school then go back and continue my education, in Tampa, Florida. Well; I went to Jerry and I mentioned my plans to him, for some reason he did not agree with the idea of me going away for school.

Questions he ask me was, why couldn't I stay in Philadelphia and continue my education and why do I need to go all the way to Tampa, FL to continue my education? My answer to him was "I need to do this for me and I feel that's what I have to do, so that I can be happy and for me to concentrate more on my education"

Therefore Jerry felt the best way for him to stop me from going away for school was to ask me to marry him. As for me marriage is something I have in mind, but only when I feel I'm ready. Plus after getting to know him I didn't want to rush into anything, so that I won't have to regret later-on. For that reason I didn't agree to marry him.

If you ask me was Jerry ready? My answer to that is no, because there is a difference between planning on getting yourself ready for something and doing something because you feel you have too. Jerry thought he was ready, but I could tell by the way he'd talk that he wasn't sure if he was ready for marriage. He felt he had to ask me to marry him just to stop me from going away for school. But what he did not understand was; he does not have to do things that he's not ready for.

"Sometimes things may look or sound pretty to do at a present time and all probably will work out only if you are ready or sure about it. And if not then what ever it is might causes you misery in your future" Yes; Jerry did love me, but my mind was set to follow my dreams and what I believe in. jerry refused to let me live those dreams. And with him acting jealous over petty things had me feeling that, I would never be able to follow my dreams the way I needed if I marry him.

When you think about it, you can say maybe Jerry really loved me but in a strange way, which is why maybe Jerry and I was not meant to be. Perhaps our relationship was a lesson for both of us. The problem was, Jerry was in love with me and I loved him but was not in love with him. I can only say, I was not the one for him and he was not the one for me, we just didn't fit to each other. I just needed to meet a guy like Jerry to lecture me about love.

Perhaps I can say knowing Jerry was the best thing that happened to me, and he had achieved a big part of my life. From his good qualities; I can tell when a man really cares for me or not. I have recognized how it feels when you're in love with someone and that person who you're in love with does not feel the same for you. Well Jerry was in love with me in his own way and there was no way I could have changed who he was and that's why, we did not last.

After my relationship with Jerry was over, my objective was to continue with my plans and wait to find the type of guy who can really support my dreams, the type of guy who I can fit with and respect my decisions, the guy who will understand me.

Chapter3

Personal experience

A year and couple months later, all before I had to move from Philadelphia to Tampa Bay for school I met a guy name jimmy. Jimmy was also trying to pursue his goals. Jimmy was a guy who loved to speak his mind "sometime too much" Jimmy was a good guy but long distance relationship was not his thing.

This guy was very impressive at first, everything felt so right, even when I had mentioned to him I was going away for school he never tried to stop me or neither change my mind about it. He was also a guy who respects my decisions. Even when he would not agree with them, he'd let me make my own decisions. At the beginning he treated me just the way a woman would want to be treated by a man. He respected me, cared for me, loved me, and trusted me.

My relationship with Jimmy was different. We usually got mad at each other then later on it was like nothing happened. Sometime, I did things to get him upset and he did things to get me upset. But we only stayed mad at each other for two or three days and then we'd go back and forgive each other. When he acted like he does want to speak to me, I'd always try my best to have him talk to me! Another way of saying "We'd always try to make up to each other"

The beginning was magnificent, isn't always? Well; I guess it would have been different if I did not have to go away for school. But anyway I had to do what's best for me.

Jimmy and I started having problem just when time was approaching for me to go away for school. On top of everything, not only I was falling in love but also my heart was telling me jimmy was the man for me.

His attitude was unpredictable, he stopped calling me on the phone the way he used to, therefore I decided to hide my feelings for him and left Pennsylvania with no words. When I got to Tampa, FL I decided to forget about Jimmy and not call him. And trust me that decision was hard to make, but I had to do it. The only thing I had in my mind was if he's the one for me then he would come around.

After a while being in Tampa, Florida; out of no where I found out from a friend of mine name Ed that Jimmy was asking for me. I decided to call Jimmy to find out what was going on, when I called Jimmy; he expressed his feelings to me and he got me understand the reason why he was acting the way he was.

Unfortunately I understood; and tried to work things out. I knew this time was going to be a long-distance relationship, therefore I tried my very best to understand him and be patient with him. Again everything started fine and my feelings were rushing back to me. There we go again; things went back to square-one, just when I thought Jimmy and I could actually have something real. He stopped calling again and when I would call him he would act like he had nothing to do with me or he would ignore my phone calls.

One day Jimmy and I were having conversations over the phone and he started telling me "he's crazy about me, and cares for me a lot but he's not good or strong enough to handle a long-distance relationship". Basically he asked me to move-on but wanted to still be friends,

"He never tried too hard to impress me, like other guys would do just to get my attention" He would always tell me what I needed to hear not what I wanted to hear. Funny that may sound, I did like that about him, I did like the fact he was always being himself with me.

His actions were telling me there was another female in his life. Things were started to change in a bad way, and his affections for me didn't exist anymore. When phone calls decrease to 1% and visitation started to be impossible; it's about that time to realize there's a problem. Some people will tell you like it is, some will it cool, and some would just want you to find out on your own and get the clue, "because either they might not want to hurt your feeling or not a man or a woman enough to tell you, therefore you have to find your values" well; me on the other hand I made a mistake, because even when I knew there was another female, I still didn't want to assume anything, I chose to ask question. I asked him if there was someone else? Well, his answer was no, and I asked him what was the problem? Then his answer was "I know we tried but I just can't handle long-distance relationships" The question I asked myself was, why he came back to me and yet he still couldn't make up his mind? Still; I was crazy in love; therefore moving-on was hard for me to do.

Some of my friend thought I was doing too much over Jimmy and some thought, if I really loved him and cared for him then the best thing was to agree on being his friend. I tried that and ladies and gentlemen that didn't work. My feelings for jimmy were too strong and my heart would not allow me to be just his friend. I can't be just friend with someone I'm truly in love with.

I heard people say, seeing other people would help you get over someone you love. To me it's pointless not a solution, because I tried it and it didn't work. Letting myself getting to know this guy name Tony, but after I realized I was only pretending to love him, I had to make an end of it and deal with my feelings for jimmy until it goes away. "I don't want to hurt someone else, I know how that pain feels"

I have to tell you; I had deep feelings for Jimmy, there was no stopping. I did not want to mislead him; I loved him and did not want to leave his sight. I was never scared or ashamed to let the world know how much Jimmy meant to me.

My heart was giving me the feeling that Jimmy was the one; only my mind was judging his actions toward me. It's true sometime your heart can claim something that's totally wrong for you, but if you had listened to your mind then you could have stopped yourself from making a fool out you. But how could you have known, because a lot of people follow their heart not their minds.

I was crazy in love with Jimmy where sometimes I would have in mind to go back to Pennsylvania just to be with him the way things were. But I knew this was something that my emotion wanting me to do. And deep down I knew Jimmy would of never wanted me to come back home just because of him.

I know what I want and need in life; Jimmy was a want and was also a need to satisfy my heart, but I also wanted both him and to pursue my goals. Well, after finding out he wasn't picturing things the way I was, then I decided even when I still had feeling for him I just have to live with my feelings and continue do what's best.

I thought I was getting support from Jimmy 100% on doing what's best for me, but I realized because we were too far apart his support was decreasing. Part of my dream; was to finish my education and get myself together which was what I came to Florida for. I also had in mind no matter how far my dreams take me; I was still expecting him to be a part of it. It's so droll how sometime your plans don't actually happen the way you planned it.

Jimmy probably thought the long distance was only hard on him. But the truth is, it was also hard on me, because I could not see him whenever I wanted, I could not even talk to him because he was always busy. The only difference between me and him was, I was willing to commit myself to him and he wasn't, and I was willing to try to make it work and be true to him. All I ever wanted from Jimmy was his support and his love, but that could never be possible because he wasn't ready to commit himself for a serious relationship.

Sometime I felt I was trying too much and was not getting the something in return. I felt like an idiot, because I knew I was only invisible to him but yet I still found it hard for me to make the choice I needed to make "which was moving on and get over it. It just that, every time Jimmy and I talked, I felt that we were still in a relationship." But finally, on a Sunday morning after church I got home and I was thinking to myself it was time for a change and time to let my heart be free and let go. I realized I have to stop embarrassing myself because I deserve the very best in love and good things from a relationship; Even when I love him I have to move-on, I just have to accept the situation, let go and let him makes up his mind. After all; "it's not fair to wait on someone you not really sure of"

I have no reason to blame jimmy for his weakness on the long distance relationship. Like I said before, he never asked me to wait on him; he was honest and told me he's not able to handle long distance relationship. I'm the one who had hard time to accept it. Well, I accept it in my mind but my heart refused to accept the situation. Now that I'm older, I realize I had to go through petty or hard situations just to make me who I'm today.

When someone doesn't love you the way you love him or her and you don't feel needed; you must put down that relationship and move-on with your life. Even when you truly love that person, that person may not be the one you need to spend your life with. Sometime true love doesn't come true, only because you might be the only one who's willing to give your heart to that other person.

It's not possible to find someone the way you want them to be 100% (your way), but it's possible to find someone the way you need them to be. Someone who would understand you and who will always help finding solutions when you both are facing problems. From my experience I learned you can never change someone's bad manners or someone's immoral ways, especially if that person does not have any attention on changing his or her own bad manners or not even willing to work it out with you. Its true no one's perfect, but keep in mind we all should at least attempt to be.

Chapter 4

"3 main reasons long-distance relationships cause problems to some people"

First reason is, because sometime the **memories that you guys share**. Second reason is **someone to be there** to satisfy every need. Last reason: **Sexuality** is the big reason why long distance relationship causes a problem to some people. And yes; I said it.

Some people refuse to understand sex should not be the only way to build a relationship. A relationship should be built on commitment, devotion, trust, patience and love. With all these four things you can go anywhere around the world to achieve anything, and you two would support each other with nothing to worry about.

You both should acknowledge you two are belong together, and after you finish situating your life then you both would still continue to grow together and build more memories. Also, you can go back on having as much sex as you two want!

Chapter 5

Make your own choice

From time to time we all have to make choices that would benefit us, but it's up to us to be committed to these choices. For example let's say one of you chooses to go away for school or go away for any other necessary reason; and your mate does not approve or maybe acts like he or she does agree but when really he or she doesn't, either way it's up to you to come up with a decision. The decision can either be, you accept to stay because of him or she or you go. It's a choice that you would have to make.

It should be up to you if you want to change your mind about going away for what ever reason it might be or not. In my opinion, I don't think anyone should change their dreams and plans for anyone else. It has to be your choice and your commitment, because you don't want to wonder about where you would have been in life if you had followed your decision.

If your mate has problem with encouraging you and feels that he or she would not be able to handle the long-distance relationship then you should let it go. From that point if they come around, then it's up to your heart, mind and past history together to tell you if you should go back and continue having a relationship with that person again.

Even when it's a hard choice to make, you have to do it for you. And anyway; if you and that person were destined to be together, you two will always be. There's no such thing as putting your life and dreams on hold for someone else. You both should support each others' dreams and decisions. That's the way it should be. Just know; your soul-mate should encourage you to find success, just like you should encourage them on finding the same no matter how far one of you have to go.

Life sometimes wants you to go elsewhere to find who and what you really are about. Sometimes you have to go elsewhere, where there's a better chance to achieve a task that's very important to you. If you have a chance or a second chance to make a difference with your life, then you should go for it and do not let anyone hold you back. Of course; you can achieve anything no matter were you at, but sometime you have to go out there just to find the real you. You were born for a purpose and your purpose probably elsewhere and to find that purpose you have to go seek for it. It's very important to follow your instinct when ever it tells you to take a chance, because opportunities come once in your life time.

See I know some other people who were in long-distance relationships and made it. First example, a male friend of mine who I knew from back in high-school had decided to go away for college. His girl friend stays home and went to college as well. After they had finished their education, they're both decided to get married and settle down.

Another example, I knew this girl who has a baby by her boy-friend; and her boy-friend wanted to continue his education in a different state. After he had finish with his education, him and his girl now happily married and have another child together.

What about those soldiers who have to travel 1000 of 1000 miles away from their husband, wife and children? Some of them have no idea how long they have to be away for.

I'm sure they don't like the situation, but they have to do what needs to get done and what they dedicated their lives for. Some of them may choose to do it because of their situation in life and some of them may also choose to do it because it just something they want to do.

Most of them I believe have family, I mean; husband, wife, and children. Most of these people still try to find a way to keep their relationship together. Majority of their family support them and understand the situation and help them pray to return home save every time they have to leave for a war.

Of course these people probably have some ups and downs because of the situation, but the point is; they're committed to each other and willing to make it work. What I'm try to say is when two people are meant to be, nothing will be able to break that bond and that attraction will never fade-away. No matter what the circumstances might be, you both would always find ways to communicate and make it work with no excuses what so ever.

Chapter 6

<u>**Stop forcing it**</u>

When a relationship does not work out it had to do with one of you in the relationship or both of you. Normally one of you is the cause of why the relationship cannot work-out, but anyway; We're all refusing to accept the truth and always blame one or the other for each others' stupidity and still remain in that blinding spot that causes us not to think about reality.

Truth is; when you have problems in a relationship, it can probably means two things; maybe your relationship is being testing or you two are perhaps not meant for each other. To find out is not to force it just let it go and let destiny takes place.

For example; let's say one of you are cheating and the other person founds out, from that point, the one who had cheat would be the one causing the end of the relationship. And if for any reason both of you decide to cheat on each other, then both of you would be the cause that would make this relationship became a total mess. Therefore this relationship will never last, because there is no sincerity that can build this relationship and it is because of both of you.

When you're ready to make a relationship work and the other person doesn't feel the same, does not make that person's terrible, arrogant; loser or whatever names you might think of, it just means you and that person just doesn't belong together or he/ she just not the one. Perhaps that person may not be ready for you and it might be time to stop wasting your time on that person. "Clear and simple"

Chapter 7

<u>**Soul-mate**</u>

I know when we need something we work for it and fighting for it, but some of us seem to forget when something bringing pain and suffering it doesn't worth fighting for. When the person is the right one, you both will realize how much you love each other and will give each other respect with out having to fight for it.

Rich or poor; we all need some kind of relationship in our lives. It can either be a devoted relationship or a relationship that just debate on sex. Everyone's difference with different belief and different mentality, but there's some people out there who are really looking forward to spend their lives with someone special and there's also some people who just don't care, it's what ever to them. "Well, I think everyone needs a special person to spend his or her lives with, but it takes time for you to find that person" You have to take your time and be patient for the good one to come to you. Most of all you have to let God choose for you, because when you keep choosing for yourself you'll get lost and confused, and instead of going forward you'll go backwards, trust me I learned that the hard way.

However when you do find that one, they will be ready for you and understand you. And you'll find out all your bad relationships were just lessons to help you grow-older, wiser, brighter, and stronger.

There's time for everything. You can be in a relationship with someone and that person may not be the one you for you. This is why when you in relationship you always have to pay close attention to benefit you, first to see if that person is the one and not with you just to play games. Believe it or not, your heart and their actions to you will help you identify. After you find out then the choice is yours to make.

Chapter 8

<u>All men and women are not the same</u>

Never say all men and all women are the same, because there's lot of goods men and women out there who's willing to bring goods for females and males. These men and women are just too good; that's why they're hard to find.

Unfortunately they are some men and women out there who just want what they are looking for from you and run. There's a possibility you just have to go through some bad relationships before you can run off to your king or queen. But it does not have to be that way, if you take your time and let God direct your soul-mate to you.

Some men and women are just not ready for a serious relationship or not to settle down, therefore it's up to you if you want to go along with their games or not, well; believe it or not you do have an option. If you're ready for a serious relationship then you most let it go and stop yourself from getting hurt, and when they're serious then they will come back to you for good and will be ready for you. From there you will be able to tell if it's meant to be. And if they never come back then it just an experience you probably needed to go through to help you develop.

Sometime we throw things away out of anger and then later when we settle down and calm ourselves, that's when we see the exact way we should have acted. When we run back to get it then it's too late, that's why we should not let anger takes control over you and you should think ahead before making any decision.

Chapter 9

<u>Let love be love</u>

Like my father used to say; in a relationship there should be trust, honesty and communication no matter what one of them may have done. My father once told me "the good and beautiful feeling you have coming from your heart toward someone else, it's what we call love and love is what and who you have passion for" says my father "the question is how we willing to identify that passion? Be very careful of what you're asking for and what you wish for, as they can become your nightmare"

I think love is a great feeling, but you have to be very careful of who you are falling in love with. Don't love anyone because they got money. And honestly, when you love someone for money, you don't really love them because there's no passion from you for that person, you just using that person for opportunities.

Truly love a person for whom and what he/she is. For some people money is everything, but they forget that everything's not money. Most people get married to the wrong person or for the wrong reason and of course they end up divorcing. It's something you and I don't have any control over. Someone can offer you money, but ask yourself can the person offer true love or both? I'm talking about someone who is devoted to you, and respect you in general. Respect is another feeling that can help you acknowledge how much you really worth, and helps you go on. When you're too much in love with the wrong person, sometime blinds you up from seeing the truth about that person. That's why you need to get to know the person better before you give your heart to them.

Some people just know the exact thing to do or say to keep you blind. The best thing is, when you find that person who is devoted to you it's for you to be willing to do the same and let destiny controls and be smart enough to not letting yourself get play by any players.

When your man or your woman trusts you, you got to respect that and trust them too. However if you cannot trust them then there's a serious problem, and you need to find out what it is because both of you should trust each other. Logically man will always be men and women will always be women, the whole thing is for you to know when your man or your woman truly loves you and not play with your heart.

Keep in mind if your man or your woman having trouble trusted you then the relationship won't last. When a man or a woman act jealous for you in some condition it's understandable, but when they go out of control with their jealousy that can cause physical abuse or other negative reactions.

Chapter 10

Abuse is not part of love

Physical, verbal or any other type of abuse are wrong no excuses. If you think it's O.K. when a man or a woman lay hands on you then you're wrong. Even when it was only one time, believe me if he or she did it once and you don't take any action, you best believe he or she will keep doing it over and over. A man or a woman should never laid hands on you by physically hurting you, and you should never make up excuses for someone who is abusing you.

When someone truly loves you, they will never try to hurt you. The best thing they'd do is communicate with you. Exactly; I say it; "communicate" just to find solution. And if after that communication you two cannot come up with a solution to work out what ever the problem might be, then you both should come up with a final decision to stop wasting each others' time.

In life you should not have to force anyone or anything that refuses to belong to you, and if you do it might costs your life. When your mate does you wrong then you have to let them make it up to you, at the same point in time; if you're the one who done anything wrong then you have to do anything that possible to make it up to them.
A true man or a true woman knows when they're wrong and knows the best way or the best thing to do to make it right to you. I understand no man or woman is perfect, but I believe every male or female should at least try to do what's right.
I think it's always best to be close friend with your partner. Have a little fun together, don't be too uptight, and if your partner is uptight then loose them up! I mean have some good time together, joke around sometime and live life the way you two should.

Chapter 11

<u>What type of guy or woman are you looking for?</u>

I met the controlling, jealous, the careless and the user type of guy. But I always know deep in my heart the type of guy I'm looking to spend my life with.

You got to find yourself a man or a woman who can fulfill your soul, your mind and your needs. It's always better to have the type of man or woman who trusts you no matter what and it's your job to not betray that trust. A man or a woman who knows what kind a man or a woman he/she has. In another of saying he/she should know who he/she's dealing with. The type of man or woman who will not empty your pocket for no necessary reasons!

The type who loves you for you, the type of man or woman who respects you in general, the type of man/woman who's not a gold digger, the type of man/woman who can help you save, the type of man or woman who respect his or herself, the type of man or woman who's intelligent, the type of man or woman who's not too controlling, and the type of man or woman who you can call true man or true woman in every ways.

Kind of man or woman, who's not using you for money, the kind of man or woman who pictures life the same way you do, who knows when, how, and where to express his or her feelings, not waiting for you to beg them for anything, has goods coming out of his or her mind, can help you find your way to build a good life for you and for him or herself.

Chapter 12

Feelings

I know when you're in love with a person and that person finds it hard to believe or abuse your love that can be very stressful, especially when there's nothing you can really do about it. I know it terrible seeing someone you truly love with someone else, especially when you can't tell that person how you feel about them.

It's aggravated when you're really looking for something serious with a person but that person refuse to let his or her heart fall for you or refuse to see how much you truly care for them. I learned you can't just live with the feelings you have for someone, you just have to express them to that person you love. But just remember when two people are feeling the same about each other, all these stressing, hurts, and aggravations will not exist.

It's true, it's ashamed when you're spending all of your time thinking about someone you love, but that person does not even taking 10 second out of their time to think about you. It silly and tiring when you see you cannot be with the person you love because of some confusion or because of petty situations.

It hurts knowing the person you're truly love does not even love you the same or acting stupid toward you. It stupid when you see you're willing to give all of you and that person does not want it.

It hurts when your heart is burning out for someone you truly love but then again that person has no idea. And when you actually try to stop loving that person and that love just won't go way. It hurts when you finally found someone you actually thought could be the one and eventually proves you wrong. It hurts seeing your true love escaped from your life. It hurts knowing you had it good, but then you let it escaped.

That's why we have to learn from our errors and take our time to build a better one next time. The most important thing to know is; when a love is accurate there's no hurt, because love is not suppose to hurt.

Chapter 13

<u>Love doesn't hurt</u>

Love means; showing great care to a person or thing that one loves. It is a deep romantic or sexual attachment to someone and an intense feeling of deep affection. Love is how we choose to identify it. Love will always stay love; no matter how we describe it. Love is love. Just like there's no other description for hate.

Some people say love hurts. Some say love stinks. Some say there's no such thing as been in love. Some say there's no destiny. But I'd say love is how we choose to use it.

The significance of love; condition of loving someone, you must accept everything about them, even their faults or weaknesses.

When you truly love someone you will want to commit to them, and if you notice you're not ready for commitment then don't used the word love because Love is not just a word, there's more to it then just telling someone you love them. You may probably like the person, but not loving the person. Liking someone doesn't mean you love them. There's a different between like and love.

To me liking someone is when you appreciate certain qualities about that person or you like that person for the type of person he/she is. And loving someone is when you feel a special passion for someone, and it's when your heart cries out loud for that person.

Chapter 14

<u>Never regret, but learn</u>

My advice to you is to let god direct you and take note from your heart before taking any action. Yes of cause; you may listen to your heart, and still make mistakes after doing what your heart told you to do. At least you will feel you didn't have an obligation to do anything.

Keep your head-up and never give-up. Men/women come and go, but your dreams can only achieve once in life time. Be independent and find your own way out. And never regret what ever you've done, just learn from them.

Chapter 15

<u>Enjoy life but plan for your future</u>

There's nothing wrong with wanting more than what you got. There's nothing wrong with wanting to be the very best. There's nothing wrong with having a big dream. Your dreams are your goals and your goals are what you need for a better future. Enjoy your life and plan for your future while you have the opportunity.

You might be young but time will not wait for you. Believe it or not; if you don't take action to prepare for your future, there will be a time where you will wish you had taken action for your future when you had the chance. Later on when you don't have anything to support your life; you'll be all alone trying the hard way to figure out how to maintain.

You don't really know where life going to take you, and no one was born ready with what and who they are. We were putting on earth by the holly God for a purpose and we're destining to become something. And it's your right to find your destiny. Also; when you see your destiny it's not exactly what you dreamed up, you can always change it.

What you only need is not to give up, keep your goals big and be rich or keep trying. Sometime it may feels that time taking you too long to achieve your dreams or even have idea to give up, just remember all these are satins' power that wants to hold your blessing. The only time we should stop trying is when you're six feet under.

I believe there's always solution for every problems, but only if you make your mind work to find out those solutions.

Do not do what other people are doing or what they want you to do. Do what your heart wishes you to do. At the same time, keep in mind to think twice before you make any decision. Because when you think twice before you act, it gives you a chance to find out if what you had in mind was what you really wanted to do.

Chapter 16

<u>My country</u>

I never understood why some Haitian teens were ashamed of where they came from or ashamed to say they are Haitian. But what these young Haitians and other young people who are ashamed of their country don't seem to understand is that they are the future of their country and they have to make a difference to be proud of whom they Are.

We are all human regardless of where we come from or regardless of how different we think. As for me even though I have Dominican background, I was more around my Haitian family. Therefore I identify myself as Haitian.

As I was getting older I started being aware of why these teems were shamed to say they were Haitians, and it's only because a majority of people look down on other nations and make other nation feel and look inferior.

In my opinion, I think it's always better to help others if you can, instead of criticizing. You have an opportunity to shop, dress up and enjoy life anytime you feel like it. Perhaps you should be thanking God for giving you these opportunities and help or pray for those who don't have opportunities you have.

Those unhealthy countries and people need to use the intelligence God created them with to help manage and take charge of their own country. They need to keep their hopes-up and understand everything rich people and countries are capable of doing that they can achieve the same, but only if they use their knowledge, stick together and understand they're the only one that can change their country for the best.

I believe in traveling around the world and finding out more about other countries, instead of sitting around listing to false accusations or misunderstood script and judging. if I cannot afford those trips, I read and learn more about their culture. When you learn more about other cultures, you find out the most interesting things you never knew before.

Let me share a bit of my culture with you. For some of you who probably don't know anything about my little poor country. And those who sometimes believe on what they see on TV; everything is not what they seem. In Haiti's history, I found out from my grand parents that Haiti is more than a tropical country and more than a poor country. Haiti is the poorest country in the world, but what some of us seem to forget is that there's poverty in every country; however some of them may have more resources to better themselves.

My grand parents once told me that Haiti used to be call The Jewel of the Antilles; Haiti was the richest colony in the entire world. In the 1750 Haiti supplies as much as 50% of the Gross National Product of France. Haiti used to product sugar, coffee, cocoa, tobacco, and cotton, the dye indigo and other exotic products. You might question; how did The Jewel of the Antilles was once wealthy and today becomes the poorest country in the world? And how this country was once creative but today is half desolate? Haitian governments have always been the cause of Haitians misery.

I believe the main person who has what it takes to aid a country is the president of the country. However some presidents think being a president is just about the title or it just a beautiful title they should own, but have no idea of what it takes to be a president or don't know the true meaning of being a president. Because most of them are not doing the job that they're suppose to be doing for their populations.

They think they know what they're doing and when 95% of the habitants are unhappy: physically, financially, most of all security. For example; People shouldn't have to leave their country and embarrassed themselves because of circumstances, they should want to leave it by choice.

Haitian women in Haiti depend on their child to help financially. In Haiti some parents believe on taking care of their child when they're baby and once the child grow up then their children have to taking care of them, therefore they depending on their child. That's the reason why they believe on keep having kids, and this country is too small to carry all these people.

In Haiti there is different class of population. There's high class, middle class, low class and lower class.

High class people are those who have high education and excellent jobs, but still want more instead of helping their country. The middle class people are those who are knowledgeable, but just have a job enough to survive.

Low class people are those who are poor and don't have a good job to help support their families. However with the little knowledge they have, they try to build their own just to have a place to sleep. And the lower class people are those who are extremely poor, they are sleeping on the street, have no food to eat, and willing to do any type of work to survive; because they don't know how to read and write.

Chapter 17

<u>Voodoo</u>

Some citizens in other country believe every Haitians or Africans serve voodoo; however it's not necessary true. A lot of Haitians or Africans believe in gospel (Christianity) and who also take their religions very serious. We as Africans we just like to let what we done seen openly instead of hidden them or keep them a secret.

Of cause, voodoo is a black religious cult practiced in the Caribbean and the southern US, combining elements of Roman Catholic ritual with traditional African rites, and characterized by sorcery and spirit possession but that doesn't mean very Haitians or Africans believe in it. As for me; my parents had raise me to believe in my savior Jesus Christ the holly spirit.

For those who think voodoo is a religion; well, Voodoo is a religion for those who believe in it. At the same time; those who believe in voodoo, practice it to do goods and some time to do bad if necessary, on the other hand others some of them practice it only to do bad. For others who don't understand what is voodoo may think it's all about negativity, it's like I said; it's depend on how those who believe in it; practice it.

The most important thing we need to understand is that 75% of people in Haiti believe in Christianity. And Voodoo is not the case of Haitians misery if you wondered.

Chapter 18

<u>To all my Haitians and to other Nation</u>

For my Haitians and others who're probably reading this book. I'd love for you keep in mind to always stick together, Stop the violence, stop the hatreds, stop the back stabbing, and stop the selfishness. Build your own, stop breaking down what you build up.

Start making your own profit, stop depend on others, start claiming what's yours, stop claiming what's not yours. Help keep your country clean together, stop looking on other people. Start taking good example from others instead of the bad examples, stop talking about each other in negative ways, and stop doing wrong things to others.

You have to make peace in your country, no one else will or can. Don't wastes today's best; save some today's best another to have in tomorrow's misery.

Chapter 19

<u>Insensitivity</u>

What causes people to hate each other? Why is there division in some families? My answers to these questions are money, jealousy, misunderstanding and negative appearance. Money is usually the big issue and sometimes some people just choose to hate.

Some individuals really have courage to destroy their own mothers, fathers, brothers, sisters, husbands, wives, daughters, sons, uncles, aunts, grand parents and friends for money. It's ashamed to see other people are taking others' lives away just for something their can always work hard for to own.

Of course you need money to survive in this world, that's why you have to work to make it, at the same time don't let it make you. Don't let it spend you, and don't let it take control over you. What's money any way? Money is not evil; it's the people who give money too much importance that are evil. Money doesn't have to take control over you if you don't let it.

Put yourself in those people that are being victim for what ever and asks yourself, would like it if that was you? Question, if someone pick-up a weapon to hurt you what would you do? I bet you'll be ready to run or ready to fight back to defend yourself; only because you know it will hurt and it's not a good to get hurt.

You and I both know; you would never want to die and getting kill by anyone. Perhaps if you can stay a life for ever you'd love it. Therefore, why doing something to others when you will not want them to do it to you?

Chapter 20

Things that we need to accomplish

Devoted to accomplish these things:

Follow your heart

Focus on your dreams

Stop playing games with other peoples' emotion, heart and mind

Express your feeling to the one you love

Let go of things that are hurting you

Respect others

Help god by bringing more souls to him not by chasing them away from him.

"If you have Jesus into your live and you want others to accept him into their lives, then you need to be around them to demonstrate how good Jesus really is, not by staying away from them"

Treat others the same way you would actually want them to treat you

Help others if you have the opportunities

Help others in any other way you can, even when you don't have money to give

Let your mate find his/her destiny if you truly love them

Stop prejudging

Stop looking or talking down on other people

Stop abusing other people

Find help when you need it

Don't let anyone break you apart

Don't expect everyone to like you or what you have accomplish

Find who you truly are

Know yourself first

Continue loving those who love you

Still love those who wish the wrong for you

Do not fear to go after what's important to you

Stay positive

Think positive

Make a difference

Chapter 21

Poem: Why do I love him?

My heart can't take it anymore;
His games are driving me insane.
His speech proves he doesn't care anymore. His actions show no love;
but still my heart wants to keep him inside.

Why do I love him?
Its clear enough;
There is no more affection,
There's no more love from his eyes.
There's no more love from his heart for me, but yet my heart still wants to keep
him inside.

Why do I love him?
I'm saying to myself; my feelings are truly real, but how could I still have true
feelings for someone who doesn't understand meaning of love? I give myself
many reasons to let go, but my heart still wants to keep him inside.

Why do I love him?
It's killing me inside; it hurts.
It's hard to focus; it's undesirable.
I want to let go; in my mind it's possible, but in my heart it's unstoppable.

What kind of love is this?

Why do I love him; when he doesn't even care? Why do I still love him; when he
runs out of love for me?
Silly me; yes, I know it
Silly love; where does it come from?

Poem: Life

Life is what you create
Born to survive. Live to experience sadness. Struggle is a part of life.

Stand up in the middle of trouble,
Hope and fight until your dreams come true. Learn how to make your own
decisions. Disappointment is a way to find accomplishment.

Know what you Want and Need
Succeed your goals. Peace with those who cause you pain. Find you own
happiness. Sickness is a possibility of death. Who are we? We are gulp of air.
And without air there's no we,
this is life, face it.

Poem: Patience

Patient goes along with being able to tolerate, being able to accept and being able to keep up and choose

we choose to tolerate those who're around us. We choose to accept and to deal with whom ever and what ever we have to deal with. We choose to keep up and to be patience with everything or anything in life

Patience is what we need to make it.
Patience is a gift that been given to us, to feel proud of things we took time to get done.
Patience is the hardest but the greatest of all.

<u>Poem: Who am I?</u>

A woman who god created to become all she can become.

Who am I?

Passionate woman

romantic woman

loveable woman

woman who been through enough, and who's fighting for her way out. Woman who just wants to be her

Who am I?

Tired of stress

tired of living other peoples' dreams

deserve to make herself happy

Woman who's looking for self-determination, because she deserves it

Woman who's independent and proud

A woman who's not letting anyone break her apart

Who am I?

Woman who not scare of getting hurt

And if she does; then she'll learn from it and make the best of it.

A woman who got her head on her shoulders and refuses to give up. This is who I'm

Tell me; who are you?

Appreciation

I want to thank God for making this opportunity possible, and want to thank him for creating me to make a difference in life. Also thank him for who I'm and for creating me with my faith.

Shout-out to my baby-sister Muriel, my baby-brother Jean-Marc, my mother Noelzina Boursiquot, my cousins, and special thanks to my aunty viergelie Boursiquot for everything she done for me. Special thanks to my cousins Laurent meteryer.

Big thanks to my special friends, Janail Glover, Tiffany Simon, and Edward; who were also supporting and encouraging me to publish this book and to continue to focus on my agenda and go after my dreams.

Thank you to everyone who's supporting this book and who believes in me. And big thanks to my publisher who make this opportunity possible

About the Author

Ermitha Gracia is a young adult who was born in Haiti and has a Dominican Republic background from your fathers' side and raised in Brooklyn New York. Later on she moved to Philadelphia, Pennsylvania. Ermitha graduated from Fels high school in Philadelphia. She owns a degree in Medical Office Management and now she currently resides in Tampa Florida continues her education. Ermitha is working on her modeling career and other talent. She's working on her next book, and working on her poems book. To find Ermitha Gracia poems, search at welovepoems.com.

Ermitha loves writing and her stories are base on her experiences and the knowledge that was once giving to her by her father George Gracia. Ermitha Gracia enjoys dancing because she believes dancing can also be a good and healthy way to keep her body in shape. Ermitha is working on opening a restaurant and planning to open a retail store in the fashion industry. Ermitha Gracia always wanted to inspire all teens and to have them realize they are the future. Ermitha gracia is a simple young woman who is trying to make a difference, lives her dreams also to find her purpose for being a life.

Ermitha is the oldest child out of third children from her mothers' side and the only child from her fathers'. Her families aren't rich but they always try to live a natural life by striving for achievement. Says Ermitha "she will never fail to remember where God brought her from, because if it wasn't because of where she came from, she would never be here today to make a difference in life".

978-0-595-39647-4
0-595-39647-X

www.ingramcontent.com/pod-product-compliance
Lightning Source LLC
Chambersburg PA
CBHW050335290526
45785CB00006B/2508